# Cloister

# Books

Cloister books are inspired by the monastic custom of walking slowly and reading or meditating in the monastery cloister, a place of silence, centering, and calm. Within these pages you will find a similar space in which to pray and reflect on the presence of God.

# Sabbath Keeping

# Sabbath Keeping

# Donna Schaper

COWLEY PUBLICATIONS

*Cambridge* ✦ *Boston*
*Massachusetts*

Published in the United States of America by Cowley
Publications, a division of the Society of St. John the
Evangelist. No portion of this book may be repro-
duced, stored in or introduced into a retrieval system,
or transmitted, in any form or by any means—including photocopying—without the prior written permission of Cowley Publications, except in the case of brief
quotations embodied in critical articles and reviews.
Library of Congress Cataloging-in-Publication Data:
Schaper, Donna.

   Sabbath keeping/Donna Schaper.

      p.       cm.
   Includes bibliographic references.
   ISBN 1-56101-163-0 (alk. paper)
   1. Sabbath. I. Title.
BV111.S325 1999
263'.2—dc21                   98-48343
                                      CIP

Cynthia Shattuck, editor;
Vicki Black, copyeditor and designer
This book is printed on recycled, acid-free paper and
was produced in Canada.

Second printing

*Cowley Publications   •   28 Temple Place*
*Boston, Massachusetts 02111*
*800-225-1534   •   http://www.cowley.org*

To the Rev. Dr. Bennie Whiten,
my friend and my boss,
who knows well
how to work and play.

# Contents

# Preface

I am keenly aware of the need for sabbath keeping because everywhere I go people urge me to go faster, to do more. My spiritual credentials for writing this book are simply that I yearn to hear more deeply God's message to slow down, and that like many others in our culture I continually hear the opposite message as well. My credentials are also domestic ones: we have three children, and are a family with three adults—my husband, myself, and a woman we "adopted" and who adopted us many years ago—three cats, two dogs, a dozen chickens, a small farm, a mortgage and two car loans, and a nearly hilarious life. Some days, one of us remembers to pick up the milk!

Keeping sabbath keeps me sane. I walk, pray, sing, garden, worship—and do so with a discipline and vigor that keeps play and praise in my life. God is good to me. Sabbath keeping is a spiritual strategy: it is a kind of judo. The world's commands are heavy; we respond with light moves. The world says work; we play. The world says go fast; we go slow. These light moves carry sabbath into our days, and God into our lives.

Our culture urges us to think that we need more of just about everything. In fact, we need less. That is the premise of this book on sabbath keeping: more is less. Keeping sabbath is a conscious choice to restrict input. It is a decision not to work in all the available time, but rather intentionally to play in some of the time we have. Keeping sabbath is a method for focus, rest, and play in a life otherwise dominated and tyrannized by scatteredness, fatigue, and work.

Many of us spend long parts of our life worrying about what does not matter. Like Schindler in *Schindler's List*, we get to the end and realize that we could have sold the car: we could have given away even more than we gave away. In sabbath keeping we do not give away the car so much as relinquish the control economic and cultural expectations have of us. We say "no" to a scripting of our life that is without play or rest or grace. We say "yes" to a life that is grounded in God's grace, and then we receive more than we could ever have imagined of rest and play. For sabbath keeping allows us time to love, and thus restores to us the joy of our salvation.

one

# What is Sabbath?

Sabbath is setting aside time for God. For centuries, religious institutions obeyed God's commandment to remember the sabbath day and keep it holy by making one day a week, a Saturday or a Sunday, "God's time." Jews hallowed Saturdays as the day of God's rest from creation, while Christians honored Sundays as the morning of the resurrection of Jesus.

Sabbath originated as *shabbat* in Jewish thought. It was understood to be cosmic in its source: in creating the world, God rested on the seventh day. The institution of *shabbat* is also a reversal of some of the trouble of Eden. "You will work with the sweat pouring down your face, so that the earth will barely feed you" is one of the curses of Genesis, when Adam and Eve were driven out of the garden. But on the seventh day you may rest. Sabbath is freedom from the curse of work, which was understood as blessing as well as curse by God at the beginning of creation. This both/and nature of work, as curse and blessing, became part of the conundrum of sabbath keeping.

For Jews, the emphasis of *shabbat* is on rest and playfulness. Arthur Waskow, a Jewish theologian, calls *shabbat* "the time when you stop doing...You study Torah, you sing, you dance, you celebrate, and you reflect on what the previous six days have been." He also speaks of *shabbat* as taking the world "off the easel":

> We have done this amazing painting of modernity and instead of taking it off the easel and looking at it, and learning from it, and then beginning some new project...we are still putting on brush strokes which, in fact, are making it uglier and uglier.[1]

Sabbath is taking the world off its easel. It is holy remembering. It is holy seeing. It is the pause in

---

1. Arthur Waskow, *The Witness* (January/February 1996), 23.

which we remember what has already happened. Sabbath is artistic focus.

The idea of sabbath keeping as a way of pausing fell victim to a number of internal inconsistencies over time. Work was both blessing and curse. And playfulness, all by itself, had the potential to be a curse as well. The logical difficulty in some time being allotted for God (as though all time were not God's, as though Monday belonged to someone else) quickly created sabbath struggles. Jesus asked the disciples why they should not pick corn on the sabbath: the playfulness of genuine *shabbat* can turn into religious legalism.

The poet Emily Dickinson saw the inconsistencies of sabbath keeping as Jesus did. She declared that the sabbath could be kept everywhere, all the time:

> Some keep the Sabbath going to church
> I keep it staying at home
> With a bobolink for Chorister
> and an orchard for a dome.[2]

---

2. "A Service of Song," in *Collected Poetry of Emily Dickinson* (New York: Avenel Books, 1982), 114.

Eventually the Quaker "anti-sabbatarian movement" developed to join its voice to reclaiming all time for God. The Quakers did not want their religion for Sundays only. Now the sabbath has lost even its blue law protection, and with activities scheduled and shops open seven days a week very few can really make the argument that sabbath, kept in the Christian way, rivals sabbath as the Jews and the Moslems keep it. The problems of the original blessing and curse of work keep surfacing. People cannot separate God from ordinary time, or even from the sweat of work. Not only is God inseparable from ordinary time, God also enjoys a different day in different cultures. Blue laws were too small for the sabbath: they could not protect it.

Thus the practice of observing sabbath on one particular day has fallen victim to its own internal inconsistency. If God says that both work and play are good, and human beings know how to turn even what is good into idolatry and legalism, how do we set time aside for God? Do we need one day and one day alone? What if even religious people cannot agree on the right day for God?

Our need for sabbath, for rest and time for God, does not have a one-day solution. The need for rest has only gone underground into a deep urgency and a deep desire. Even people who believe that God is with them on Monday like to worship a Sunday or Saturday God. We like ritual. We even like the help that blue laws once gave to our rituals, and often moan about the loss of even one day a week for rest. But whichever way we like to keep our sabbath and get our rest and give time to God, we know that today we live in a society that is not friendly to sabbath keeping. We work on Sundays; our children play sports on Sundays. Jews long ago who lived in cultures that did not understand or support their beliefs and religious practices knew what it meant to squeeze God into normal, everyday life, and now we Christians are discovering the same challenge.

Today many of us are more concerned about the physical impact of lost sabbath time than about its difficulties in definition. We are desperate for rest in a culture that seems to reward only effort. We understand ourselves as overworked, but in a way we are proud of our exhaustion and our failure to honor the sabbath. We know our restlessness well. Many people are not only very tired—we are sometimes even proud of our fatigue. Sabbath faces a real problem: work, not rest, is what our culture values. We may be desperate for other values and other rituals than those of work, productivity, and effort—but until we honor values other than work, we probably will not have other rituals, either. Author Toni Morrison tells us there is a difference between a ritual and a spectacle: ritual honors the truth of people's lives, while spectacle honors the falsehood. Sabbath has become a spectacle.

Sabbath keeping values our ability to rest, not merely our ability to work. In sabbath we live in God's economy, where our purpose is not production but play. In keeping sabbath we measure ourselves by a different yardstick: we try to see how much delight we can take in the world, not how much we can get "done." We can delight in how much we leave unfinished and open, a gift to God, not how much we can finish off. The poet Donald Hall says that most people live life checking things off their lists. Such list checking is the opposite of sabbath keeping: the things on our list are our life. We want to keep and savor them, not cross them off.

Is it possible that our restlessness deserves such deep judgment? Yes, but we will not get that judgment from God. Sabbath—time for God—is a gift in its origin and in its keeping. It is not another must; it is a may. God invites us to keep sabbath; God does not demand it. The third commandment, that we remember the sabbath day to keep it holy, is as much an invitation to joy as it is a law about living. It is an invitation to a party, not to a hanging. Sabbath keeping is not one more thing to add to our already long lists. Sabbath keeping is lightness, not heaviness.

One religious writer says that people ask him often for a list of "spiritual reading." Instead of a reading list, however, he offers the notion that people should do all their reading spiritually. Sabbath keeping is a way of managing all time—time for reading, time for work—spiritually. Sabbath connects what is disconnected. Sabbath is not the opposite of work, but the basis and depth of work. Monday can be God's day as well as Sunday. It is a question of perspective. We do not move from sabbath to work, or from holy days to profane days: we keep work holy and pack holiness in our bags for work. When we do not keep sabbath, our life is a list.

Sabbath is a way of living, not a thing to have or a list to complete. By observing it we become people who both work and rest, and who know why, when, and how we do either. We also recognize the occasions on which we do both at the same time. We know how to pray, how to be still, how to do nothing. Sabbath people know that "our" time is really God's time, and we are invited to live in it. We are living our eternity now—this Tuesday and Wednesday, this Saturday and Sunday.

When we keep sabbath, we pay attention to God's invitation. We separate time into parts precisely to hold time together. We know that time is our time and that our time is a gift from God. Sacred time is not when we get our work done but all time, which we keep and honor by sabbath living. We dishonor time by not taking our time. Not to keep sabbath is like receiving a beautiful gift and forgetting to say thank you. It is like staring at a banquet and complaining that there is nothing good to eat.

Theologian Heather Murray Elkins speaks of "altaring time," gazing all the way down to see the sacred at the core of the clock. She teaches us another way to wear a wristwatch, saying yes to numbers and yes to digits and yes to hands moving—and by all these affirmations saying yes to God, who is the source of time's movement.

Jews used to clean their entire house in preparation for the *shabbat*, the "Queen of Days." They prepared special dishes, special foods, and had special employees, *shabbat goyim*, who worked for them on that day. We may all need to hire one of these *goyim*: in our culture we are in need of each other to help us keep sabbath.

We can eat for our bodies or we can eat for our souls. Sabbath eating is to delight in our food, feasting and not merely eating. Ordinary meals contain grace. I carry a basket instead of a briefcase, and in it I keep a beautiful mug and spoon so I do not have to eat and drink from plastic or paper. I am keeping sabbath by using beautiful containers. Do I think this basket is God? No, and neither is the mug. But they transport me out of my time into God's time; they remind me of God's promise that time is beautiful, that the point of time is to "altar time." I "altar time" when I carry my basket and my mug even though I am still on the road, still drinking coffee brewed by a multinational corporation. Instead of altering, I altar. I give the time to God.

*Spirit of the Living God, help me this day to focus my attention on what really matters. Keep the fragments of this long day together, and as it ends, let me see my part in its parts, my connection in its connections, my life's way in its many ways. When I get confused, clarify me. When I get lost, find me. And when I wonder what meaning all the pieces have, visit me. Confidently, in the name of Your Son, who knew the threat of the fragments to the whole, I say Amen.*

## two

# Sabbath in the Wilderness

Sabbath keeping is so easy that it is terribly hard. We are all doing too much, and we know it is not enough; we cannot do more, but we know we must. Our gaze is unfocused, our expressions weary and worn. Our faces have taken on a wintry, snowed-in look as if we were in the wilderness. Time has become like a blizzard: it is snowing, and then snowing some more, and we do not need reminders to keep our shovels ready. Chipping ice is something most people have to do year round. The idea that we *should* rest is almost cruel.

The book of Numbers, which recounts the tale of the children of Israel's forty years of wandering in the wilderness, tells a bleak story about the penalty for breaking the sabbath. A man is discovered picking up sticks on the sabbath, working when he should have been resting. Since any work on that day is forbidden by law, they bring him before Moses and the whole congregation stones him to death outside the camp (Numbers 15:32-36).

This story is about the people of God trying to remain a distinctive people. They have to keep the sabbath their way. They can permit no deviation. The story in Numbers goes on to command the people to make fringes on the corners of their garments, each with a blue cord, "so that, when you see it, you will remember all the commandments of the LORD and do them....and you shall be holy to your God" (vv. 37-40). They must "fringe" their garment so that people know they belong to the one God.

Oddly, this text gives us a good account of the monotony of wilderness time, that time which so deeply resembles some of our own. We know we must remain distinctive, together, faithful, marked as the people of God. We know we must rest. We must be peaceful. But in our culture, in our way of life, we do not know how to avoid picking up a few sticks on the sabbath. Or we have a double set of marching orders—to keep sabbath and to pick up sticks. We live in the monotony of this double bind of required rest and required work, cold and bored and captive in the wilderness. We do not need to stone each other; we stone ourselves.

Much of the book of Numbers is the story of the census, in which every male Israelite over twenty years of age is numbered, first those who went into the wilderness and died there, and then those who came out of the wilderness and saw the new land. Numbers is the story of the new generation and the old generation. It gives us case law, including what to avoid on the sabbath and what to wear on your clothes. Even these minor themes have an impact on our own contemporary wandering. They help to structure the experience of wilderness and tell a tale of how we might get out.

In our own day we would never stone anyone for violating the sabbath because we would not have to. In our own violations of the sabbath—our Sunday soccer games, our wide open malls, our unwillingness to rest, to stop, to give it a break, we stone ourselves daily. It may not look like stoning, but ask almost anyone you know about their spiritual condition and they will tell you, "Exhausted—bombarded—under the gun—burned out!" The ancient monks called this condition *acedia*. Bored to death while being bombarded with stimulation.

Modern *acedia* is the result of violating the sabbath and living in a culture on permanent fast-forward. It pretends to be the real world, the real way, the way life is meant to be, as though God were cruel enough to ordain it that way. God is not that cruel. God ordains another ontology, one in which we fringe our garments and pick up sticks six days a week, but not seven. In God's ontology, we can rest.

The culture itself is monotonous, an endless walk in the wilderness that seems to lead nowhere but back to new and colder versions of Egypt. We all know the monotony of obeying our marching orders. Monotony is the name of our wilderness, a place that is simultaneously enormous and cramped, a world where the orders are clear: Move on. Move up. Make more money.

Keep on going even if long ago you forgot where you were going. You get off an airplane in Orlando and cannot tell if you are in Oakland or Chicago. The television looks the same although you could swear you turned the channel. Who needs stones?

Put a fringe on your garment, Numbers advises, "so you shall remember and do all my commandments, and you shall be holy to your God. I am the LORD your God, who brought you out of the land of Egypt, to be your God" (15:40-41). People may think you are crazy or somewhat "different" for keeping sabbath in a genuine way. The passage advises us to be different—and not a little, but a lot. Not merely in the simple keeping of a ritual sabbath, but in the complex of differences that mark Christians as people of faith. This sense of difference says, "I may be in the wilderness, but I am also awaiting the promised land. I may live here beside you and send my children to the same schools and shop at the same stores, but I am on my way to a better land. I am on my way. I keep sabbath."

To keep sabbath, we have to do so little. Add the tiniest piece of embroidery to the garment of

Christ and you add color to a dull world. Take a little sabbath. Give it a break, even one afternoon a week, and you have done something quite damaging to the monotony. As strong as the monoculture looks, it is really quite vulnerable. Talk to people who already do wear the cross embroidered somewhere on their lives, who already do things differently. Watch how the best among us have managed to live in their friendship with Christ. They take time off from work—sometimes it is Sundays, sometimes Tuesdays, but they are not always *on*. They tithe. They give thanks at meals. They take the strangers in. They take the picture off the easel. They altar time. They hope for things that other people do not hope for. They live in God's time.

Not everyone has to wear fringe. But we do need ways to remind ourselves and each other that God created a better world than a wilderness of double-binds. We need rituals and reminders to keep sabbath. We need to tend and keep our confidence. Keeping sabbath is a way of confidence keeping: confidence that the land we see is on the other side of the wilderness, and that it is very warm there. Sabbath is living in God's time, in God's way, in God's promised land.

Many wish that they could keep sabbath the old way, on Sundays, with a fine family dinner after Mom, Dad, and the two kids have attended church together. In this nostalgic myth, the children are very quiet and well-behaved in church. They have Sunday shoes and wear them willingly. Mom makes homemade gravy to go on the mashed potatoes. The afternoon is as long as heaven. Leftovers, or something cold and simple, come out around dinner time. You had a sneaky feeling that even Protestant Moms and Dads made love, as Jews recommend, as a sabbath *mitzvah.* But of course you did not know.

We know what has happened to this long, good day. Less than a quarter of Americans live this way. Mom does not know how to make gravy, although Dad may make a sauce. Most children cannot be pried out of their sneakers. Many people have to work on Sunday, and very few people think that Christians should have their sabbath day singled out in a way that neither Jews nor Moslems do.

The fact that Sunday as we used to know it is gone does not mean that we can no longer keep sabbath or no longer wear a fringe on our garments. We may find other ways to set time aside for God. We may find other ways to keep away from the sticks we have to pick up to heat our homes and feed our children. Keeping sabbath is a decidedly different way of living: it is deeply counter-cultural. It is living out an intentional witness, a resistance to the way things are. When we live differently, we live with God.

If we are lucky, we can probably still keep a Sunday-long sabbath. If we can, we should. But if we are not so lucky, we will find other ways to keep sabbath. There are many ways to fringe our garments.

*If earth has grown too old around us,*
*and spirit grown too weak within us,*
*if joy has fled from our house*
*and hope abandoned our hearts,*
*come Lord Jesus. Be our guest.*

*Let thy gifts to us be blessed.*
*And let us dig down below our fatigue*
*to the places where the water flows.*
*Send us back to work lighter, fully watered,*
*dried up no more.*
*Accept us, again and again.*
*Through Jesus Christ our Lord. Amen.*

### three

# The Music of Sabbath

I sat on a bus one afternoon and watched a child hum himself to sleep. His rhythm was impeccable. He was tired and taking a little rest, using his "hum" as a bridge from wakefulness to sleep. He was keeping a child's sabbath.

More than one person uses music to keep the sabbath's heartbeat alive. In fact, if you think you cannot keep sabbath, or do not know how, just think of how you immerse yourself in music. Follow that path and you will not need to find sabbath. The sabbath will find you.

I was raised on music and the name of my music was Bach. The hymns of my youth in a Missouri Synod Lutheran Church still come back to me if I have a long line to stand in or a big painting job or a long car trip. I am astonished at how many hymns I can sing, all three verses. The same is true of rock-and-roll—start any of the fifties or sixties ditties and I can probably sing the whole thing for you. These hymns and songs are a bridge from the ordinary to the extraordinary. They turn regular time into special time by keeping time, by keeping the beat.

Many of us think we are not religious, but that is not the case. Rather, we are pre-religious. We hum or sing and forget about ourselves for a while. We find the path to God. When we become aware that we are making space for God in our space, and time for God in our time, we are keeping the beat. We are keeping sabbath. We have become (sneakily) religious.

For me, the best time for keeping sabbath with music is in the car, when I am alone and no one can hear my singing. My tape deck and local public radio station are my best friends. The music loosens up the knots. It smoothes me out. If I am not piping in music, I am putting it out. I can always tell if I am in a good mood: I am humming. When I am in these moods, I join all those who are making space for God in their space, making time for God's time in their time. These strategies are like Russian dolls: one fits inside the other, which in turn fits inside another, just as God's time is the core and the container of our time.

Music gives us a sense that we are in touch with the deeper parts of our lives. It solves our double bind of needing to rest and needing to work at the same time—sometimes we *can* do both. Even if we cannot solve the bind by both working and resting at the same time, music can dissolve the conflict and tension we experience. Music lets us see how nested and held and contained we are; it shows us how our lives connect with other people's lives. Music resembles sabbath in the way that it separates from regular time: it brings us to time set aside for God.

One pundit says it this way: "If a man were permitted to make all the ballads, he need not care who should make the laws of a nation. I would rather control a people's ballads than their politics." That is certainly true. The ballads contain the politics in a way that the politics could never contain the ballads. The ballads become a container, a bowl, for the work and the tension.

Music holds us like a bed, or a couch, or a pillow. It carries us in a way that nothing else can. So does sabbath. Each receives our fatigue. Each nests our fatigue. Each gives us a "lift," a way to carry ourselves without getting so tired from our own weight. We are upheld by music. Music keeps sabbath, reminding us that all time is God's.

Watch how many people swarm to singalongs of the *Messiah* at Christmas time. Even my Jewish husband has his own score, which he brings to as many churches as he can in December. Imagine the revitalizing of our churches if we could get these same people who lust for choral music to sing in our choirs. Music lifts us above the pedestrian, during the big holidays or on the smallest days. I think more people worship in church for the sake of the music than for anything else. Even when the sermons miss their point, we can find God in the singing. Cultures change slowly but they change most dramatically with regard to music. People will put up with liturgical innovation, even with bad preaching, but they do not like their music to change unless they have a part in the changing of it.

People find music precious. When they cannot rest any other way, when they cannot find God any other way, they can find God through music. Thus the odd conservatism about changes in hymnody: people are desperate for rest and for God. They do not want anyone taking away their last, best hope. We have lost so much else that transports us to God that, by God, we do not want anyone interfering with our music.

We do not have to be so afraid. God can come to us in a Bach concerto, an Ella Fitzgerald croon, or a Leadbelly jig. God can use all kinds of music, including sacred music, to put us in the mind of eternity. Often people who are angry about changes in traditional church music are actually angry about something else. Sabbath is booking a trip to eternity, and they fear they will lose their ticket. So the more diverse our worshiping communities become, the harder it is for people to find their tickets. The more despondent they become about music, the further out of reach God (or faith in God, or church) seems. Ask any teenager: they cannot worship God through other people's music. They need to worship God through their own—and they will, and do, in churches or outside of them. Teenagers are not just buying CDs; they are also buying tickets to eternity.

Once I conducted an Arab-Italian wedding at my church in New York. We had a few Moslem prayers, a few Catholic prayers, and I was the liturgical midpoint. There were three flower girls in velvet. The father of the bride was more than a little tipsy when he got to the service. After things had gone on for a while and he figured out we were almost done with the service, he stood up and demanded, "Where the hell is the *Ave Maria*?" At this point, the organist went right into it with great strength of song in her voice and in the organ. Everyone cried. We had a wedding. We had the emotional meltdown we had come for. People took their rest in the middle of the great anxiety that is "wedding" in America. The music allowed it to happen.

As a parish pastor, I have long enjoyed the ancient prayer, "O Lord, preserve the music makers, let their hands be supple on compliant strings." It speaks of the genuine appreciation that the music makers deserve. But the church needs to be very careful not to weaken the sabbath by restricting access to it: more than one music can allow us to set aside time for God. How can we keep the old music from strangling the new music as it tries to be born? Keeping sabbath with music is sometimes hard for us because of the battles that have broken out between traditional and contemporary sacred music. Nevertheless, on the other side of these battles is a beautiful eternity. When we cannot find the words or patterns to sing with each other, we can always hum...until the tune comes round again.

Theologian Harvey Cox tells a painful story of being forbidden to play his saxophone in church as a child. The exclusion of his music meant that *he* was excluded—not only from church but also from God. Many others could tell the same story of the church, as guardian of the sabbath, keeping them out. When that happens, people are damaged severely. They think there is no sacred time for them. They think that God is not for them, but for other people with other kinds of music.

We can keep sabbath with music by loving the music we have. We can sing our songs and play them on whatever instrument we have. I will never forget my grandmother playing her hymns after dinner when she was genuinely relaxed. She was with God in these moments. Sometimes now when I sneak glimpses of my daughter dancing to her music alone in her bedroom, when she has forgotten to close her door, I realize her ecstasy. Her music takes her there. A great Tao saying observes, "All the fish needs to do is to get lost in water; all man needs to do is to get lost in the Tao." I would not be surprised to find out that the Tao is music.

In *Meditations on a D Major Scale*, musician Bertha May Nicholson speaks of how much she loves good music and how much she hates bad music. She goes on to say, however, that the more deeply she understands good music, the more capable she is of seeing inferior music as useful. It opens her up to the beat in people. Good music comes from "just music," after all. Luciano Pavarotti did not start out magnificent; he *became* magnificent. We do not need to be any more skilled than the child with his thumb to use music to keep sabbath. One of the points of music is its populism. Anyone can keep the beat anywhere, anytime. There are no experts. You can hum badly and keep just as good a sabbath as Pavarotti does.

When people fuss over liturgy or prayers or hymnody, they are really talking about keeping a more beautiful sabbath. It was St. Paul who reminded us that when we were children, we hummed and thought and spoke like children, but when we became adults we put away childish things. Keeping time for the sabbath becomes increasingly sophisticated because we want to keep it better and better, so delighted are we that God's time is so rich in and through us. We may fuss. We may get our prayers and our notes just right. Only when we become self-righteous in defense of our excellence do we err from God and the sabbath. When we fuss over music for the sake of sabbath rest, we have no problem; when it is a way to avoid the peace of God, we do. Then we have simply rationalized our distance from God.

A colleague of the missionary physician and music scholar Albert Schweitzer tells the story of being near the African equator and hearing a Bach toccata wafting down the Ogowe River at dawn. It was eighty-six-year-old Albert Schweitzer practicing on his zinc-clad pedal piano with the intensity of someone who was rehearsing for a gala recital in the jungle scheduled for that afternoon. The man went to work for Schweitzer in the jungle, so moved was he by Schweitzer's music. Music makes some go to war, it makes some melt down, it makes many cry. For me, music keeps sabbath. It carries me, it lets me rest.

In *Underground Harmonies* Susie Tannenbaum writes of music in the subways of New York, where we have "the ultimate New York City paradox, in the dingiest of spaces, a paradigm of beauty."[1] We can keep sabbath on Sundays at the cathedral at Chartres, with the best organ, the best tradition, and the most humble priests. We can also keep sabbath if we are stuck in the Los Angeles airport and everyone has left but the custodian, who is humming, "I'm in the autumn of my days." We can keep sabbath in the jungle and we can keep it in Jerusalem.

If the spirit does not always move us, sometimes a simple piety, like the doxology before dinner or a chant at dawn, can keep us regularly focused on the power of God in music. Gregorian chant is the music that brings me home on late

---

1. Susie Tanenbaum, *Underground Harmonies: Music and Politics in the Subways of New York* (Ithaca, N.Y.: Cornell University Press, 1995), 302.

nights from faraway meetings. The more we sing anything, the more deeply it carries us to God and God to us. Deciding what song will be sung at our own funeral is a good way to prepare to die. I insist on "My Lord, What a Morning." It helps me to know that such a promise will accompany my transfer to the other side.

One day I want to be a subway sax player, or a cellist at the Louvre in Paris. I will join that little boy who knew how to put himself to sleep. I will put myself on permanent rest. I will keep sabbath in this life and the next.

*When in our music God is glorified,*
*and adoration leaves no room for pride,*
*it is as though the whole creation cried*
*Alleluia!*

*How often, making music, we have found*
*a new dimension in the world of sound,*
*as worship moved us to a more profound*
*Alleluia!*

*Let every instrument be tuned for praise!*
  *Let all rejoice who have a voice to raise!*
*And may God give us faith to sing always*
    *Alleluia!*[2]

---

2. Hymn 420 in *The Hymnal 1982;* words by F. Pratt Green.

four

# Decluttering as Sabbath

Decluttering is clearing away the less important things on behalf of the more important things. Decluttering gets down to what matters, spiritually as well as physically. You cannot make dinner with yesterday's dishes still clogging the sink, nor can you keep sabbath if too many worries clutter its gate.

When we fail to make decisions about what really matters to us, choosing fog over focus, waffling over decision, aimlessness over intention, we become people who do not know how to keep sabbath. Instead, we keep clutter. Not to decide on a life of focus is to decide on a life of fog, choosing confusion over clarity.

One of the best guides I have found in determining life purpose is by businessman Stephen Covey. His book, called *The Seven Habits of Highly Effective People,* includes exercises about writing a life mission or purpose statement. He recommends a mission statement that is simple, sustainable, and personal. When we know what we must do, rather than letting others decide for us, then we can also decide what we do not have to do. Of course, we should be "successful." But at what? The former poet-in-residence of Boeing Corporation, David Whyte, tells us in one of his poems, "Give up everything to which you do not belong." The choices we make in determining our life purpose and life focus involve giving up everything to which we do not belong. These choices focus our lives. They monogram our towels. They sign our name to our life.

Oddly enough, the more successful we think we are at sabbath keeping, the more serious are the temptations that get in God's way. Sometimes our very talents can get in the way, as an old story tells us. A great organist is playing a masterful concert. At the end of the first set, he discovers that not only is he supremely pleased with his performance but the crowd has risen to its feet in a cascade of bravos. He is moved to speech: "Yes," says he, "that was my best performance ever." As he speaks, the custodian who has been in charge of blowing the air into the pipes of the magnificent organ joins him on stage. "Yes," he adds, "this is our most magnificent performance ever." The maestro is aghast. "What do you mean *we?* Did you attend music school? Did you practice every day? Did you reach deep into your soul to evoke that music?" The custodian slinks offstage.

But when the maestro returns to play his second set, he places his hands on the keys and his feet on the pedals and nothing happens. No music comes out. He tries again and still nothing happens. Everyone in the audience realizes what has happened at the same moment: the custodian is not providing any air.

The maestro is not stupid. He sees how he has cluttered himself with his own triumphs. He has no room for others, let alone for God. Promptly the maestro stands up to thank the custodian for his labor and his faithfulness over the years. He returns to the bench. He places his hands on the keys and his feet on the pedals and magnificent music emerges once again.

Like the maestro, we need to remember where our air comes from. We need to remember whose air we play. Our lives are cluttered by our own performances, our own skills, our own powers. These good things get in the way of something even better—the ability to remember God, the source of our air.

This story about music could be told about almost any one of us. Sometimes we lose our way; we get buried in the clutter of the small and insignificant. Sometimes we have no spirit—or, in the Korean phrase, we lose our "salt." We play music without soul and keep appointments without spirit.

Our lives become cluttered with our accomplishments, our degrees, our need to practice for our next performance. Good things pile on top of good things, which pile on top of still more good things. We get cluttered by the good! We have a hard time remembering from whence our air, our breath, our buoyancy, our generosity comes. Keeping sabbath pauses us. It pauses us before we play our concert or go out to work. It refreshes us after our concert and before we go to sleep. On Sundays or Saturdays, at worship we remember the source of our air, making it less likely that we will offend God or our custodians. We dedicate our talents to God. We do not take all the bows ourselves.

Decluttering is not austerity. It is not getting rid of everything so that we have space for God. It may be rearranging things so that they are in right relationship to God, so that "tidying" is not our life's work but rather an opening to God. We open in sabbath deeply enough and often enough so that we can return, refreshed, to a messy room or an undone project.

Some people can keep their weeks and their work focused by weekly worship, while others need more frequent times set aside for God. For sabbath is not merely going to church on Sunday; it is remembering the source of our air, which we can do any day. It is a spiritual decluttering, the way we must clear a coffee table that still has last week's newspapers, tickets, Kleenex, and earrings spread all over it.

Sabbath is like homing, a return to the place from which we have come so that we may go out again with vigor. When work weeks were more regular, Sunday morning accomplished the homing pattern for many. Now that work weeks are more chaotic and schedules more varied, we need more frequent reminders of God. Although we are desperate for the homing action of sabbath, we will have to attack the clutter of our lives in new ways.

We can clean out our cars and remove "yesterday" and we can do the same thing with our lives. We can move on. We do the small things as a way of reminding ourselves to do the larger thing. We remember our air. We refuse to be buried in debris. We sweep out the toast crumbs and keep sabbath with a clean table and a clean soul. I hate any morning that does not give me a long moment of sweeping out the kitchen before I leave for work. I feel rushed. I miss the time to thank God for children and breakfast dishes and breakfast smells. I miss the time to thank God that I have work that is full and useful. The broom is my way of moving between work and home: I rest in it.

Sweeping the floor and cleaning out the closet can be highly spiritual acts. All too often, we put the word "spiritual" on a pedestal and keep it far removed from our ordinary lives. Our cars and our tables are connected to our souls and our souls are connected to our cars and tables; we are not divided. If we are cluttered in one realm, we will be cluttered in another.

In our normal weeks, we become discombobulated as things pile up. The coffee table joins the counter in becoming the place of unopened mail, unpaid bills, scarves worn once, old newspapers that were never read. In sabbath we clean spiritual house. We declutter and start over, letting go of things that are urgent on behalf of things that are important. If we solve problems all day long we will not get to what is important until five in the afternoon, when we are too tired to pay real attention. The rest of the day we are fiddling with problems caused by what we did not do yesterday. Instead of starting every day solving the problems caused by what we did not get to yesterday, we could begin the day working ahead, living ahead, living as though we are the people we say we want to be.

Living this way will be different for everyone. I start the day by shaving it, cutting out what will be too much. That usually means making no more than about a dozen phone calls and making sure they are the ones that are essential for today. Another goal I have is to confuse my work and play. I like to play at work and work at play. These "confusions" amuse me. A third is to experience the holiness of marriage and family, which means I have to locate the time to enjoy my family. A fourth is to remember the poor in some concrete way. A fifth is to thank God, so that I do not forget where my air comes from.

These personal missions and goals change from time to time. I do not meet them so much as *practice* them. They are directions, spiritual strategies, spiritual goals. In keeping them, I keep myself from being so busy making up for yesterday that I cannot even imagine tomorrow. I declutter by putting a few things at the center so that the rest falls away.

When we are cluttered, we spend time worrying about lost or missing things. When we declutter, we worry less. One summer my husband lost a ring I had given him. It was a ring with three small diamonds in it, reminding him of each of our three children. He caught a hard fly ball during a softball game, jammed his finger, removed the ring, and put it in his pocket—or so he thought. The ring never showed up, even though we have wasted a lot of time looking for it.

But every time we tell the story of the lost diamonds, we remember our love for each other. We recite it. We ritualize it. The ring is gone in the same way that the corn was eaten by a hungry man on the sabbath, against all the rules. It should not have happened, but we remember what the lost ring points to rather than what it is. The ring points to our love; the corn pointed to the sabbath law. We can ruin the sabbath with rules, but we can also keep sabbath by keeping the rules in an unruly way.

Sabbath living is often helped by the simple act of taking time to look at things differently. In a big storm on the first of April one year, the snow was so heavy that our old deck collapsed. It had been built on the base of the old barn and for months we worried about how we were going to replace that huge deck for the three thousand dollars the insurance company gave us. Finally, we saw the light: we did not need to make the new deck the same as the old deck! It could be smaller.

It could be different. It could be itself. When we had the time to get the old frame of the old deck out of our way, we saw everything differently. We achieved a useful clarity. The new deck is beautiful: it sits just right on the hill.

In the same way, sabbath ritual gives us time to remember. It gives us the clarity we need to see what is going on. Too often our days are so filled with old thoughts and old images that we would not know a new or creative thought if we tripped over it. Sabbath clears the mind.

When we keep sabbath, we find that we do not live in a cramped or cluttered place after all. Instead, we live spaciously, where doors are open all around us and the air blows fresh and free. Like our deck, the space we live in sits just right on the hill. We are at home with ourselves and at home with our God.

*So little is clear. So much is fuzzy. Bring us to clarity, God. Lift one layer of confusion and clutter so that we may see. Show us how we use*

*confusion to keep from moving. Give us a deeper appreciation of complexity—and from there let us see all the lights that you have put at the end of our tunnel. Remind us of all the times we have been lost before—and of all the times you have already found us. Through Jesus Christ, our path and core. Amen.*

five

# Sabbath Prayer

One way we make time for God is by preparing a place for ourselves to wait upon God. Jesus knew this pattern well—the sabbath pattern of exile and return, of homelessness and home. He made a very strange promise to his people, given that he was a man without an address, a man without a home, when he told people, "In my Father's house there are many dwelling places....I go to prepare a place for you" (John 14:2). A homeless man promises his people a home. An austere man promises abundance. A simple man promises a multistory dwelling.

In sabbath we go to a prepared place. We imitate Jesus' preparation of place by preparing our own. The prepared place is a mansion; it is many rooms. It is ample. It is spacious. And it is uncluttered. This image of an uncluttered mansion is one that is hard for us to understand. It mixes much and little, abstinence and plenty, centeredness and sprawl. With Jesus, these kinds of mixtures often happen: he surprises us with a sabbath spirituality that is not what we had assumed it would be.

Prayer is the most traditional of sabbath keepers. Prayer practices the presence of God. It pays attention to God as part of life. Whether in grace before meals, or in morning and evening prayers, or in prayers for a specific purpose, prayer keeps sabbath. It sets aside time for God in the midst of time for other purposes. It can be words of petition or praise, a breath, a sigh, or a laugh.

Prayer allows us to dive deeply into any given moment. Prayer allows us pause, allows us to be where we are. More important, prayer brings a sense of proportion, a sense of being in one place rather than another, of being here and not there. Instead of living in the past, deep in remorse over what might have been, prayer helps us hold onto our capacity to remember. Instead of living in the future, plotting and fuming about what might yet be, we retain the capacity to prophesy. We live in the present with memory and with hope. We do not load minutes with more than they can bear. We live, here, now, knowing we have been somewhere before and are still on our way.

Prayers are nods or bows to mark our time. Prayer furnishes a kind of pause at critical moments during days and at critical moments in life's emotional swings. The essayist Noelle Oxenhandler writes:

> I love the word pause....Such a time represents a kind of time that is vanishing: a floating time, completely free of usefulness, suspended between wakefulness and sleep. This is the time zone of wonder, when we fall out of the habitual, the taken-for-granted, and are startled by what is.

She remembers the special seasons of the church year in her childhood as a series of pauses:

> When I was a girl, the season of Lent had a mysterious power all its own. It was the power of interiority...forty days of rock and sky....But increasingly we live in the twenty-four-hour time of commerce, of convenience. It is 7-Eleven time, the fluorescent

time of unmodulated, shadowless light, where coffee and doughnuts are available at all hours, where the rhythm of breakfast, lunch, and dinner has no meaning, and where Sunday is Monday....The twenty-four-hour availability of that which we crave does not really provide pleasure.[1]

Modern people are desperately in need of rituals for quiet. Spiritual and bodily disciplines both quiet us, and in the quiet we practice the presence of God. It is said that in the past people slept longer than we do. Before electric light, they slept twelve hours a day with plenty of time for different kinds of sleep, for dreams, for meditations, for just lying there. When we talk of keeping sabbath through the quiet of meditation, we might even mean the quiet of deep sleep, the kind that God visited often upon the ancients. Like Jacob or Joseph or the many others to whom God spoke in dreams, whenever we slow down long enough for God to visit, we are both practicing and inviting the presence of God.

Harried parents today, rushing from home to work to home again, for whom both home and

---

1.  *The New Yorker* (June 16, 1977), 36.

work feel the same, speak of wanting time *off*, time to "float," time to suspend reality of one kind on behalf of another. Prayer can suspend time, make it float. Probably most of us cannot sleep any longer than we do, but we can find ways during our days to suspend time and to disrupt the sameness of time on behalf of something sacred.

One of the ways we disrupt time on behalf of the sacred is with weekly worship. The better sabbaths involve communal prayers, like church on Sunday morning for Christians and synagogue worship for a Jew. These prayers have a great capacity for memory and for hope. They are also the way our culture gives us permission to live as a people, with a history and a future.

But as with many other aspects of modern life, the capacity for traditional weekly worship to be an occasion of sabbath keeping is changing. When people who go to church regularly are asked how and when they rest each week, they do not automatically reply, "church on Sunday morning," which is more and more perceived as work and obligation. Instead, they rest by hiking, housecleaning, gardening, eating a meal with friends in a ritual way. They refresh themselves outside of religious ritual. If they do choose to attend services on Sunday, they have to make a place for it in their lives; life is simply too cluttered to permit easy sabbath observance.

It is also true that more and more of us think we cannot with integrity join a worshiping community. This loss of faith in religious institutions has made the need for sabbath very pressing. Some turn to their own families for their communities, even though families are often too fragile to bear the trust that sabbath wants to keep.

Even so, families who take the time to pray together develop a sense of proportion about their lives that is missing from families who do not. Families who pray together are "clefted," held in the hands of a larger reality. The hymn "Rock of Ages, Cleft for Me" thanks God for holding and clefting us. Families who can pray together find their right size in the scheme of things, precisely because they understand that God's scheme is the scheme of things that matters.

Any number of patterns for prayer can keep sabbath. A quiet prayer before we eat. A communal prayer before we eat. A morning prayer and an evening prayer. A prayer when we leave our driveway. A prayer when we come back into our driveway. A prayer when we drive over the bridge on our way to work and again on our way home. A prayer during the first or last ten minutes of our lunch hour.

We have to be very careful not to overcomplicate prayer. Saying many prayers is often not as good as saying a few, especially when we have them memorized. With children, a single short prayer is better than a long wordy one. Lighting one candle before eating adds a physical act to an evening prayer which is simple and profound. Piling prayer upon prayer, or gesture upon gesture, is an offense to ritual. Simplicity is the key.

How do we remember God in the family? How do we convince our children that they are held by God's strong arms as well as our own? Three simple ways come to mind. Each is a sabbath on its own; each pauses in time for God's time. Each keeps sabbath by separating out our time and blending it into God's time. Each tracks normal family reality, like eating and sleeping and remaining connected to one another.

One is the art and act of grace at table. Families pray in thanksgiving for their food a million different ways. In our family we use a hand grace that asks God to be with us at our table and "all around us." Some families thank God "even for the vegetables." Others use a gathering ritual and ask the children what good thing they want to give thanks for that happened during the day. Still others use the Hebrew blessings. It matters less what we do when we pray at table than that we take the time to do it. Otherwise we can too easily forget that the food came from God, not from the kitchen.

I remember the first time my children asked me if we "had" to pray over a meal in a restaurant. I was on the verge of saying no when I said yes—and then I was delighted at their relief. "Okay, but can we do the hand motions under the table instead of on top so nobody can see?" Children love ritual and breaking a ritual bothers them: try switching a child's chair at the table and you will know what I mean. When we practice ritual with children often enough, they learn to love it.

A second way of prayer is the act of going to sleep. With small children some parents pray "Now I lay me down to sleep" and perhaps change the words "If I should die before I wake" to something more reassuring. In our family, once our children are in bed we ask them if anything good has happened that day. Then we ask if anything bad has happened. Usually they say no to both, so we have to supply the thanksgiving and the regret in a short prayer of our own making.

But when they do tell us the truth of their days, we are often moved quickly to prayer: "O God, hear Isaac's sorrow over not making the basketball team...Katie's grief over the girl who was unkind to her...Jacob's sadness that he didn't get invited to Mark's birthday party." You can imagine the possibilities. Then we move to a more grateful ending to the day in a prayer of thanksgiving for the party, or the game, or the friendship. Usually your children will supply the details, but if they do not, you can always give thanks for the last macaroni and cheese.

It is important to let a child speak her own words of thanksgiving or his own words of grief. We are teaching them proportion—we are teaching them how to take big *and* little things to God in prayer. The message is double: what happens to you is important, and connecting your life to God's life is even more important. This separation of the small from the large is what sabbath keeps on a larger scale and what prayer keeps on a smaller scale. We separate and then we reconnect.

A third, less frequent way to practice prayer in the family is to be ready to pray when anything truly bad happens—to a friend, a teacher, a coach, a pet. If we have taught our family to pray, and to do so as a way of marking off special time from ordinary time, then for the rest of their lives they will know what to do when extraordinary time invades.

An important part of prayer is repetition. It allows us to repeat words in such a way that their meaning enlarges over time. Prayers that are repeated over and over again do not get used up: they get better. Experiences that get repeated over and over again do not get used up: they get better. Not everything has to be new. If we can only see or experience something once, we will live a very watery soup of a life. If we can live it over and over, we will live a rich broth.

When your child leaves home for the first time, imagine what would happen if you were able to pray a prayer you had prayed together before. The absent one would be present each time you prayed the prayer. In losses like these, we need to address God, who can bring the tears of grief and healing to our eyes. The repeating of prayers keeps sabbath best because our prayers become shields to guard us against grief over time, as well as gateways to joy.

Our prayers keep sabbath because they practice the presence of God. If there is one surefire way to keep sabbath, it is in the memorization of three prayers to be used over and over again with those whom you love. If you think you might get bored with only three, why not read a book of prayers each season? Or write one? Or learn the psalms by heart? As with physical exercise, so with spiritual exercise. If we do not make the practice of the presence of God interesting, we will soon drop out of the habit of addressing God at all. Astonishing prayers are everywhere to be found. Look around. Prayers will come to you. Or they will come out of you.

*Lord, if it is true that "in my Father's house there are many dwelling places," make sure I do not get cramped today in too small a space. Keep the doors of my heart and my work open so they can breathe and sense the breeze of your promises. In the name of the Holy Spirit. Amen.*

six

# Remembering into Sabbath

As we begin to discover some of the ways of keeping sabbath in our lives, it can be useful to think of all the ways we use the word "keeping." Some people keep graves, for example, visiting them regularly to tidy and weed them, and to plant new flowers. It is a way of paying attention to someone we love even after the person is dead. Other people keep fruits and vegetables, at harvest time putting up peaches and apples, tomatoes and beans, preserving them for winter just as their ancestors did who lived off the land. They watch for the first signs of ripeness, pick their blueberries, raspberries, and quinces, cook them slowly in a shallow copper pot, and put them on the shelf in long colorful rows as mementos of the summer. We feast off them in the dead of winter and present them as gifts to our friends.

And some people act as their brother's keeper, or their mother's or father's or child's. They are "keepers" in the way that Genesis meant the phrase, as paying proper mind and attention. We "keep" our loved ones by honoring and protecting them, by taking time to know and love them, by remembering who they are now and who they have been in the past, when they are no longer able to remember.

When we keep fruit, we preserve the sweetness. We memorize it, hold onto it through the winter months. When we keep graves, we remember the ones we love who have gone on before us. When we keep our brother or sister, we honor, recognize, and remember them. These memories are sabbath pauses and sabbath pursuits.

Memory is a key way of keeping sabbath. While not all memories keep sabbath, many do. We take time to remember in sabbath time. Often we hold onto memories by developing rituals and patterns: we visit our grandmother's grave and remember who she was, remember ourselves as a child, remember who we had hoped to be. In the solitude of the graveside we keep her memory and we keep our own, and we are less alone. Memory does not compete with the present so much as deepen it: Thomas Merton called solitude a "deepening of the present." Memory puts us into a place of deep solitude where God is most accessible. Keeping graves may have gone out of style, but many of us still sneak in and out of cemeteries for the sake of the deep solitude we can find there. I once met a friend in a cemetery in Texas where we were both out walking. I did not know him that well, but I feel I know a great deal about him now. He keeps graves in Texas, and I keep them wherever I am.

During much of the time we set aside for God we look outward, focusing on our own futures and plans, on the day ahead or the crisis at hand, but at other times we remember, going back through time and thinking about who we have been and how much we have already been given. Memory helps us to remember our childhood, our forebears, our children's childhood, helps us be our brother's keeper, helps us to be kept by others. If we move deeply enough into memory, we can find all that we are and were.

What I wanted for my fiftieth birthday was someone to clean and wash the windows so that I could see out of them again, so they would say, in matronly tones, "Donna takes care of her house." Instead, I received one of those expensive, deep-voiced radios I have coveted for years. My husband gave me a painting of the Pelham Hills, the site of our first home together. There were wonderful lunches in friends' gardens, pale pink roses from a faraway friend, eucalyptus and apple lotions from children, poetry and e-mail and funny cards, a party with sixty friends. I have friends and family who think better of me than I do of myself, and I was given the gift of remembering what I really wanted. I was kept by those who love me, remember me, know me, and I thanked God for my life.

Why do we keep memory? Because it opens us to the voice of God and those who love us. We keep memory to keep hold of our life. We keep sabbath to keep hold of our life. For example, on the twenty-fifth anniversary of my ordination I preached on Jesus' temptation in the wilderness

from the pulpit of my very first church in Tucson,
Arizona. I was deeply lonely: my husband would
not come on the trip, then my sons refused. My
daughter finally accepted, reluctantly, as long as
she could bring a friend, but now I could not pry
her and the friend away from the television set. So
there I was, full of self-pity, outside the motel in
the foothills of Tucson, eating a bag of popcorn in
the sweet February air.

And then the weather changed inside me. I be-
gan to laugh. Twenty-five years? You, alone, on
the side of the hill, looking over glittering Tucson,
all before your very feet? With a bag of popcorn
and "Clarissa Tells It All" on television? A voice
came to me reminding me of Jesus' several temptations. Power as helping the poor, power as sav-
ing the city, power as stones becoming bread. In a
gleeful voice I said, "Yes, I've done them all! I
have accepted every temptation you ever sent
me." Then I was shown where I really was. I was
not above the city at all: all I had to do was turn
and look up, and there in the foothills were the
lights in all the mountain houses. I was not alone
in my ministry. I was in the city, right in the middle of it. I thanked God that I was in the city, with

everyone else, and not isolated by my ministry. Looking down at the city was part of my temptation. True to form, I had accepted another temptation. I had misread my location. I had forgotten who I was, and where I was.

A few years ago, on vacation in Chicago, my fourteen-year-old son Isaac and I revisited Buckingham Fountain. He did not want to go: "Been there, done that" was his standard excuse. I have enjoyed this fountain on many occasions. I have drunk its colored light, its wind-spread water, its life as a pocket in the city's suit, for almost thirty years, ever since I was a student at the University of Chicago. Yes, I have been there and done that, and I love to remember being there and doing that. As part of a group of protesters being hauled to Soldier's Field to spend the night during the 1968 Democratic National Convention, my head hurting from a policeman's club, I watched the fountain as we sped by in a van on the way to our makeshift jail. I have walked around its perimeter as a young mother with a child named Isaac in a stroller, and I have enjoyed lunches next to it as a worker in the Loop. Now as a vacationer from the east, I was coming back to collect more memories.

Memories, like good sauces, deserve seconds. Keeping memory is not keeping things simple. Keeping memory is keeping things deep and layered and thick. If we have been there and done that, we will come again. The return makes the first visit interesting; the first visit counts on the return.

*Lord, you have been our refuge*
*from one generation to another.*
*Before the mountains were brought forth,*
*or the land and the earth were born,*
*from age to age you are God.*
*You turn us back to the dust and say,*
*"Go back, O child of earth."*
*For a thousand years in your sight*
*are like yesterday when it is past*
*and like a watch in the night.*
*So teach us to number our days*
*that we may apply our hearts to wisdom.*
*(Psalm 90:1-4, 12)*

seven

# Relinquishing as Sabbath

We can have what we can let go of, but we cannot have what we think we have to have. The less we think we must have, the more we may have. This is the paradox of sabbath. It lets us think about what we might let go.

If we decide to keep sabbath faithfully and regularly, we sometimes get a certain tone in our voice: "By God, I *will* keep sabbath. I *must....*" True sabbath puts a sense of "may," of permission, in our voice. We give ourselves permission to live with less—with fewer plans and decreased expectations. We allow ourselves not to know everything or want everything or have everything. When one piece of furniture leaves the room, everything in the room looks different.

An old joke goes this way. Three men who have everything decide they want more. They hear of a famous guru at the top of a mountain in the country of India. They save their money, get fit for their climb, and give up everything in order to get to him and find the real secret to life. So they climb and they climb and they climb. At the top of the mountain they come across the guru—he is short, pudgy, and not very inspiring, but still a guru.

Breathlessly they demand, "What is the secret to life?" The guru responds, "Life is like a river." The men nearly faint with fatigue and anger. They grab the guru by the throat, recount the horrible details of their journey. "You have to be kidding. We've come all the way here, through all this difficulty, and you have the nerve to say to us that life is like a river?" "All right," responds the guru, "life is not like a river."

Any sense of intensity attached to our keeping of the sabbath will get in the way of keeping sabbath. We declutter our houses and our lives to remove confusion from our path; relinquishing is something else, the absence of activity. We sit amid the clutter, the household hum of a dryer, the noise of a child's radio, the television set and the telephone, and we are at peace. Still practicing the presence of God.

In her book *Everyday Sacred* Susan Bender tells the story of a woman who moved to New York but could not stand the noise of the city. In order to keep her sanity, she decided to make the two square blocks around her apartment her home. She got to know every inch of sidewalk, every door, every shopkeeper, every neighbor: she found a way to be at home by relinquishing the whole city for her own neighborhood.

For me, losing the time set aside for my daily walk puts me in a foul mood. When I relinquish my walk gracefully, however, I often get it back again. The meeting I just could not miss turns out to be dull enough that I can slip out the back door and take a stroll. Or I can use my imagination to find the extra time that my anxiety would not let me see was there. When I relinquish *my* way, I open myself up to *God's* way.

Similarly, when we let go of our fear that we will not have our sabbath, often we find that we can have sabbath nested right in the middle of ordinary time. When we let go of our desire for a perfect sabbath, with candles and quiet and a full moon, we can even come to rejoice in the wick that will not light, the noise from down the street, and the rain clouds that cover the moon—at least for tonight.

Many of us approach sabbath with envy, imagining that our neighbors or our friends are having the sabbaths that we are not. A modern rewrite of the commandments might read, "Thou Shalt not Covet thy Neighbor's Free Time." Or thy neighbor's sabbath. Thou shalt not covet thy neighbor's life. Or job. Or children. Or garden.

Envy did not begin with the story of Naboth's vineyard, but it did get a firm push then and there. Ahab, one of the most powerful kings of Israel, coveted the vineyard of his neighbor, Naboth, and wished to turn it into a vegetable garden. He offered Naboth money, but his neighbor refused: "The LORD forbid that I should give you my ancestral inheritance." So Ahab went home "resentful and sullen," lay down on his bed, turned his face away from everyone, and refused to eat (1 Kings 21:3-4). Later the king whispered to his wife Jezebel in the cool of the evening what a nice garden Naboth had next door. His queen tweaked him, "So take it. So have it. You are the king, aren't you?" Then Jezebel wrote letters to the elders of the city in Ahab's name, ordering that Naboth be stoned to death, and confiscated the vineyard.

Ahab was indeed the king, with great wealth. He did not need to steal Naboth's vineyard, but he surrendered to Jezebel and used power the way most people do: he used it to make himself wealthier. Imagine a real king needing another vegetable garden! Real kings have real power: they can want what they have and not more, or give away what they have as well as get more.

Real power has access to real choices. Real power can cut short meetings that go on too long— or stay at the meeting and not walk today. Real power does not have to worry about missing sabbath time today, as though it would never return. Real power knows it can enjoy sabbath another time: later today or tomorrow.

Envy imagines that power has to increase constantly, but real power gives power away. Aaron Fuerstein, the fleece manufacturer in Lowell,

Massachusetts, whose factory burned down several years ago, did not have to keep his employees on the payroll during the rebuilding of the plant. But he did. He gave power away. He kept the employees on the payroll for six months after the factory had burned and while it was being rebuilt. The firm now does triple its business and loyal employees work the mill.

When factory bosses spend time on the floor, they develop communities. When department chairs make sure the professor whose wife is dying of cancer is not forced to serve on a difficult committee just because it is his turn, they use power as Jesus used power. They get rid of it; they use it for *mitzvahs*, for blessings.

Keeping sabbath may involve us in relinquishing certain kinds of power on behalf of other kinds. If we allow it, sabbath may bring us to true authority, true power. The road is that of letting go, rather than increasing. Relinquishing is a way to keep sabbath when all else fails. It is the back road, the side road, the little road.

In the cluttered places where many of us live, our moral direction slips. We see a field: we want it. We hear of a guru: we must get there. Our emptiness drives us when we do not keep sabbath; our fullness drives us when we do. Instead, we may use power the way Jesus taught us to use power. We might make our goal that of getting it, precisely to give it away. For a good king power could consist in making sure that all the Naboths of the world had good fields. A good boss could use power to strengthen the people who work for her, not herself. A good parent could use power to strengthen his children, not just himself.

In a book called *Village: Where to Live and How to Live,* Peter Megargee Brown tells us that the secret to true happiness is "to want what we have." He talks about the concept of "propinquity," which helps explain why Naboth's vineyard was so tempting to Ahab. In villages we are close to many things, but we do not have to "own" them to enjoy them. We do not have to have a perfect schedule, or house, or garden, or routine, to keep sabbath.

Gandhi spoke of justice as "not wanting what other people could not have." Sometimes we have to rush when we do not want to, because we need to meet someone else's schedule. Sometimes we have to miss our walk or our time alone or our

time to pray in order to tend to the legitimate demands others have on our time. At those times we
must relinquish our own desire for quiet or refreshment, knowing that at other times people are
relinquishing *their* desire for sabbath time in order to meet *our* needs. We can relinquish that desire because we have the power to let it go, to give
it away. Keeping sabbath helps us be in charge of
ourselves, so we can use time the way we want to.

Jesus was continually using power in a different way than most of us use it. He was perpetu-
ally keeping sabbath but keeping it his own way.
In Luke's story of the bent-over woman whom Jesus heals on the sabbath, the people in power ask
Jesus why he dares to heal on the holy day (Luke
13:10-14). He tells them, "Because I have power,
that's why. I have so much power that I can decide how to use my power. I can even give it
away."

*I am not eager, bold*
*Or strong—all that is past.*
*I am ready not to do,*
*At last, at last!*

*(St. Peter Canisius, 1521-1597)*

## eight

# Keeping Sabbath as Bodies

Some of us engage in physical activity as a way to avoid heart attacks, while others do it for the heart and the soul. Sabbath can be kept by physical exercises as much as by spiritual exercises. We can pray our way to sabbath and we can play our way to sabbath. We can declutter our way, we can relinquish our way—and we can exercise our way. Some of us cannot sit at a computer screen or in a meeting all day without becoming mightily estranged from God. I am one of them: I find that my body starts to cry out if it cannot move. Those who know the zone of running—or the zone of tennis or yoga or Tai Chi or basketball—know what I mean. There is a self-abandon in physical activity that welcomes God. Spirit is friendly to aerobics; spirit comes to us often when our bodies move out of what is cramped and tense and tight.

The new yoga classes for people over fifty may be ideal for you but anathema to your spouse. Tai Chi may be the best exercise for the parts of your body that can still stretch but they may throw your shoulder out on a regular basis. The sweaty gym may be the routine that works best for you. We can go to any of these places with the intention of setting aside time for God. When that happens, physical exercises become miniature sabbaths.

Any physical activity, including sex, can help us keep sabbath to the degree that it is about self-forgetfulness. It involves that most spiritual of patterns, the "return." Sabbath is a return to our best selves and to God's time, the time from which we originated. We are always going home in the land of spirit. We are trying to get back to where we started, circling in on our origins. We speak of orgasm as "coming": we come into home. We remember a lost union. We cease to think about ourselves for a little while and think about something larger, deeper, older.

Bodily things praise God. Our task is to keep sabbath inside our bodily lives, not outside—with our bodies and not in spite of them. Everything our bodies do can praise God. St. Paul tells us to present our bodies to God as living sacrifices, as *sacer-ficio,* "holy deeds" (Romans 12:1).

Every day we do a number of things that have become habitual to us, so why not take the habit of exercise and dedicate it to God? Let the "empty mind" of a good run be a time that is readied for God. Let the good bend of a yoga posture be a time when we remember not just our breath but that our breath is from God.

Each day I walk and I do some Tai Chi—only five postures, but I know and love them well. I feel the energy of God racing through my blood. I may do a little yoga—again just five postures, but they are enough to get me to focus on my breath. I add a few exercises of bodily alignment from the Alexander Technique, a kind of physical therapy that actors, musicians, and dancers use to keep their voices and bodies from carrying weight improperly. The technique addresses the fact that we carry our body's weight in our neck and lower back, which is why so many people have painful tension in those areas. The technique teaches us how to spread the weight to stronger parts of the body, especially the feet and the legs, as well as how to sit down, how to stand up, how to walk around. Novices are embarrassed at how much they have to relearn.

Spiritually speaking, we also need to relearn some very basic things. Our inner lives, our souls, are not the only spiritual part of us. So are our hands and our eyes, our hair and our spleens. We are all of a piece. When we overemphasize any one part of ourselves, we carry the weight wrongly, and we will begin to feel tension in those areas of our soul.

This pattern of personal movement is my body's sabbath. It is time when I am not only forestalling the aging process in my spine and heart but also adding energy and space for God to move through me. I sense the presence of God more fully when walking and moving than I ever do sitting or kneeling in prayer.

We have been estranged from our bodies because we do not have to grow our own food or carry our own water. To return to a bodily way of keeping sabbath is to know that God can be a part of anything and everything. If you want to keep sabbath, if you want to rest bodily on the seventh day, perhaps you need to walk, or dance, or jump, or lift, or carry. It sounds odd, but for modern people the idea of rest is not necessarily sitting down.

Sports are the way that many Americans observe sabbath. It helps them to rest and forget about themselves for a while. Because so many people find sports more appealing than going to church, and because they are so crowded for time, often soccer appears as the enemy of sabbath. Thus a competition develops between two excellent things: Sunday morning worship and Sunday morning sports.

As the mother of three soccer players, spring and fall, I know there are ways to work with congregations and with coaches to let the two happily coexist on a Sunday morning. You can sit your children down at the table after or before the game if it directly conflicts with church, read the day's scriptures together, and talk about them. There are ways to talk about the child's gifts on the field, in the game, that invoke the name of God. There are ways to have a sabbath family time on the field and off the field. There are ways to go to mass on Saturday night, or Baptist worship on Sunday night, or temple on Friday night, and still play soccer on Sunday morning.

Some of us love both sports and Sunday morning worship. Thus we wonder whether our bodily desire for sports conflicts with our spiritual desire for worship in community. But for many people sports are not so much a leisure activity as a sacred activity; it is not accidental that games occupy the once-sacred time slot the churches once had all to their own. We must face the fact that the churches may not be speaking the holy in a language people can understand. Sports can bring the kind of self-forgetfulness that religion used to bring—a sense of belonging that is ritual in nature. They are more like religious experience than not.

Sabbath is what some people get from soccer and what others get from Sunday services. We need both kinds of rest and enchantment in our children's lives. Keeping sabbath bodily is both very simple and very difficult to understand. We can walk to the beat of God or we can walk to the beat of the world. Or we can do both. Sabbath keepers do both. We walk deeply. We walk with God. We do not walk with God only; our bodies also come along. We love both sports and Sundays—not either but both.

Sabbath keeping puts body and spirit back together again. We are carried by God; we also carry God within us. We are embodied spirits, spiritual bodies, and when we walk that way then we keep sabbath and sabbath keeps us.

*You, O LORD, are my lamp;*
  *my God, you make my darkness bright.*
*With you I will break down an enclosure;*
  *with the help of my God I will scale any wall.*
*It is God who girds me about with strength*
  *and makes my way secure.*
*God makes me sure-footed like a deer*
  *and lets me stand firm on the heights.*
*You lengthen my stride beneath me,*
  *and my ankles do not give way.*
                    *(Psalm 18)*

nine

# Sabbath Border-Making

Surely there are at least a thousand ways to draw a picture of our life that includes the proper borders and frames. Each of us must draw our own lines, but, in the words of Tillie Olsen, sabbath makes sure we have proper margins on the page. If the margins are too wide, we get bored. Our lives are too empty; we become greedy for excitement and choose whatever comes along, whether or not it is good for us. If the margins are too narrow, we become frantic, overdone, and do not even enjoy good things.

Sabbath makes sure the page breathes. It gives us the time to ask questions of God. "What do you want from me today, God? What must I do? What can I let go? What is the true shape of my life—not the distortion, but the true shape? Who draws me? Isn't it you and me? If so, how much space do I take up on my page? How much is for you?"

These are the questions that sabbath takes the time to ask. It asks what we should keep, what we should let go, how to keep the beat, how to beat the fatigue of overdone, overdrawn, overcommitted, overcooked. Sabbath honors the body's wisdom: it tells the body to rest when it is tired. All of these actions are part of border-making, boundary keeping. They bring a sense of proportion into disproportionate lives.

We hear a lot about the word "boundaries," the maturity of knowing where I start and you stop, what is my problem and what is not. This mature sense of borders is part of sabbath keeping: we reborder our lives to include more of God and less of other people, so that we listen to God more than we listen to anyone or anything else. Sometimes we must draw hard and fast lines to keep other people and their expectations from running our lives. We try to remain people who are capable of selfless giving but not of endless self-sacrifice. We do not bleed into other people's lives or let them merge into ours. We stay separate; we use sabbath to do what the word means, to separate ourselves enough from the world so that we may connect to God. Without time set aside for God and God's directing of our lives, we become the prisoners of each other. We do what we think others want us to do rather than what God wants us to do.

We keep sabbath by making these boundaries, and sabbath is kept in the maintenance of these boundaries. These are not the fences that a farmer puts up once and for all around his property; these are fences that are in need of constant tending. Sabbath does the tending of the boundaries.

We keep sabbath to keep proportion, to get to the right size for our lives, the right margins and white space for the pages of our lives. Different people "size" their lives differently, and they may also celebrate sabbath differently. Middle-class Americans need to slow down for one set of reasons, while poor Americans may need to slow down for another. A chambermaid needs to put her feet up at night for a different reason and in a different way from a harried executive. "Keeping strong personal boundaries," after all, is a middle-class value that does not make sense to the alien, the stranger, the traveler, the poor. It is dangerous to think of keeping sabbath only as a personal discipline of separating our work and our play, of "taking care of ourselves," as the new commandment reads. If we think of keeping sabbath as a self-help exercise, we will find ourselves defeated soon enough, beached on the shoals, wondering once again why we are not "good enough" to do what we want to do, when we want to do it. Sabbath is a gift that comes when God enters our time and our time becomes God's time, not when we calibrate our own comings and goings with more precision.

Keeping sabbath is much more than a personal discipline: it is an act of faith and an act of resistance—or better, an act of faithful resistance. We resist the small gods of culture on behalf of the true God of grace. In *The Reinvention of Work,* Matthew Fox makes the case that nothing less than a complete overhaul of the social and economic order will allow sabbath its blessing. We should therefore not be surprised if self-help slogans like "slowing down" do not quite work all the time to keep our sabbath. It is politically naive to think that they might.

When we define the borders of our lives, therefore, it is very important to figure out who we are keeping out and who we are keeping in. For example, as a pastor I often decide that I work too hard and must "take time off," but that results in my not being able to be available to the people who just lost welfare checks in my community. I stop when I really should start. Making sure the poor are part of the borders I draw is crucial. If they are not, there is something wrong with my circle. God will not be there if the ones whom God especially loves are not.

Perhaps we do not need so much to "protect" our time as to release it to God, who will in turn protect us in our self-giving. There is a mathematics to generosity: the more we give, the more we are able to give. That is why the premise of boundaries is dangerous; it can make us stingy. Sabbath keepers know where they start and the other stops, where they stop and the other starts. They know boundaries but they also know the limitlessness of God.

I am told that looking with the naked eye we can see the same number of stars that we would see in a cup of sand, if each grain of sand represented one star. With an ordinary telescope, we can see enough stars to fill a bowl. With the Hubble telescope, however, we would need all the sand in the country to count all the stars. God's world is much bigger than we think, and we are much smaller than we think. We matter less than we think we do, but we also may matter more, as each star and grain of sand matters to God.

How do we connect to this largeness? By keeping sabbath, not by keeping boundaries. By making sure we do not diminish the largeness of God—or "puny-ize" it, as my son said it once when he was excluded from a soccer game. I think of his smallness in being left out of the game, of his tears that day and his word, and I remember God's promise to all the poor and the left-out. In sabbath we become capable of remembering the poor, the left-out, and all the borders that are erected against them. We hope for the day when they will come out of "their place" into ours and theirs—and we hope for the day when

God's kind of time, wholeness, and holiness, will be everywhere.

*O God, in the course of this busy life, give us times of refreshment and peace; and grant that we may so use our leisure to rebuild our bodies and renew our minds, that our spirits may be opened to the goodness of your creation; through Jesus Christ our Lord. Amen.*

*(The Book of Common Prayer)*

ten

# Slowing into Sabbath

The best way to keep sabbath is to slow down. It is to wash the dishes slowly, not frantically. It is to dress slowly, not haphazardly. It is to sweep the floor before leaving for work slowly, not anxiously. It is to be where we are now when we are there, rather than letting our time be invaded by where we are supposed to be next.

In a culture that demands more and more, faster and faster, sabbath is a spiritual form of civil disobedience. Our marching orders are to speed up. Instead, we slow down. We do so out of love for God our Creator, and out of respect for our creation. We were not made to march fast. We were made to live and love and be. These things take time.

I enjoy repeating the story of an African speaker from a World Council of Churches meeting several years ago. The moderator of the panel told him he had three minutes to make his case or a buzzer would sound. He said jovially, "Oh, no, I am an African and I take my time." Sabbath respects the slowness and anti-productivity of people who know how to slow down and take the time that is needed.

Most of us go to work every day and we come home from work every day. We do "nine to five" in some form or another. Slowing down as we leave for work and slowing down as we return home from work is a very good way to keep civil disobedience a part of our lives. Prayer is also a useful gatekeeper in entering and exiting: invocations and benedictions, just as we have in formal worship, help a lot of us know where our work day stops and our play day starts, and vice versa. Such prayers sabbath us. They keep the holy and the unholy in their proper place and in proportion to each other. These kinds of prayers—or nods, or thoughts, or simple routines of sitting—can go a long way to slow down our lives.

Sabbath is about separation. Sabbath separates our time off and our time on and likes to do so slowly. The separations are fun. Now I am here. Now I am leaving here. Then I will be there. Then I will leave there. God is with me in my going outs and my coming ins, from this day forward, even forevermore.

Sabbath *keeps* these separations, the way a soccer goalie keeps a goal or a jelly maker keeps fruit. We keep the good in and let the not-good out. We protect. We separate. We put up fences and we like them. It is not that our work is not holy or that our play necessarily is; rather, our days nest in levels and layers of holiness. We remember what is holy about our work by pausing to remember; we remember what is holy about our play by pausing to remember. Sabbath is the pause of remembrance that keeps holiness a part of our lives.

The root meaning of the word "sabbath" is to separate, as a sabbatical separates years of "time on" with a period of "time off." The commandment is to remember the sabbath day to keep it holy. We can keep parts of each of our days holy just as we try to keep one day a week holy. Keeping separations keeps proportion. All things are not the same; days are not homogenized. Time is separated into its parts, and thus proportioned. We "right-size" our time at work and we "right-size" our time at play. We remember just how small—and wonderful—our little days are in the grand scheme and time of God.

What connection has prayer to work? They often seem like strangers from opposite realms. One wears tough leather boots and plods heavily, lifting, wheezing, managing, composing. The other dances with near ballet-slipper grace, lightening all loads that come near it. Prayer is more like air; work is more like earth. Sabbath prayers connect earth and sky, plodding and dancing, tough and soft. They separate realms.

Prayer and work are both connections to God. Each is, at its best, a simple acknowledgment that nothing is separate from God. Prayer, like healthy spirituality, is the simplicity that all things bow at one throne, the throne of grace, the place where Jesus lives, deep at the heart of things, at the bottom of the layers of clutter. We can pause at each layer and enjoy it for what it is, a gift from God.

Spirituality is the knowledge of one united world, with God at the holy center. Our prayer is one spoke on this wheel, and our work is another. Rather than being opposites, they are friends.

How can we keep a sense of sabbath about our work? We can pray our way in and pray our way out. We can mark the borders with a bow to God. Perhaps our prayers will have words. Perhaps they will simply be nods.

These days I live in hotels more than I ever thought I would: hotels are part of work for me, as they are for many. I have even come to like them, in that they are sparse and clean and simple. I have learned to guard my going outs and my coming ins with little rituals to mark my take-offs and landings. Whenever I go into a hotel room, I nest by putting my things away, rather compulsively, in a similar pattern. Then, when my things are settled, I say, "Hello, little house." When I leave, I say "Goodbye, little house." Do I feel silly doing and saying these things? Yes, a little bit. But I add to my hello and goodbye a thanks to God, who gives me shelter, both at home and away. I give thanks to God who keeps me safer

than the security locks on any of my many doors
ever could.

In learning that I need these marks for my border crossings, I learned that I also need them at
home. I need to nod to God when I leave my
driveway, to give thanks for the road and for my
journey on it. When I return to my driveway, I
again nod to God and give thanks for the return
from my journey. These little rituals give a proportion to my life, marking the variety and difference and nuances of my days. These nods to God
tell me that my whole life is holy and that the holiness comes to me in different parts. These nods
sabbath me. They bring the right size to me and
my days.

We can slow almost anything down. Ask
workers who want to make a point to a recalcitrant boss. It is amazing how long garment workers can take to make one dress when they are not
quite on strike but want to be. It is amazing how
long a child can take to clean a room if she does
not want to—or if she is enjoying it. Slowing is the
opposite of hastening; hastening is what we are
supposed to do, according to our culture. It is not
what we are supposed to do according to our

God. Remember the sabbath day to keep it holy, says the commandment. Do not hasten to the sabbath, just remember it. Remembering is a mighty slow thing to do. An expert can take all day.

Consider housekeeping as a way to slow down. We can keep a house too clean, and we can let a house go. We can tidy at the time when we should be letting be, and we can let be when we should be tidying. We can fail to appreciate the beauty of a messy coffee table, with leftover joy from the night before. Or we can enter Christmas with the bittersweet still hanging and arrive at Easter with the mistletoe still up.

I learned some of this sense of the delicacy of seasons and housekeeping when my eldest son went away to boarding school. Isaac was fourteen; within days his voice had dropped, and before he left he decided to redo his room. He threw out "boy" and moved in "teen." Video games, stuffed animals, guns, rockets, and large print books were replaced by CDs, science fiction novels, a computer, and an alarm clock. After he left, I insisted on cleaning out his room right after he had already done so. I kept some old wooden trains that looked too "baby" to him; I threw out an old stuffed monkey. Isaac's pet bear, "Cuddles," long lost under the bed, came out during this major interior redecoration. Cuddles is having a hard time with Isaac's maturing, as you might imagine, or at least he gave me a way to tell Isaac that I was. My tears over the bear were just what I needed.

I was not cleaning his room at all. I was separating Isaac the teen from Isaac the boy. I was remembering Isaac's boy-ness and letting it go. I was decluttering and preparing for a new focus in my life as a parent. Isaac was my firstborn son. I did not know what was coming next for me or for him. But I knew a long and slow preparation was in order, for both of us.

The morning of the day that I made a mess of the room, or so my ex-boy/now-teen told me, I had also destroyed a spider's web. The light was slant and fall-like, and I could see the web in its full complexity only because it was 7 A.M. in the garden. Just at that moment, light from the east found it and exposed it. I found the web breathtaking and beautiful. I enjoyed it for a long morning time, ten minutes of not weeding or clipping. Then I decided to clean and weed and fix around the area where it had spun its glory. I was not going to get too close to its delicate and precarious beauty.

You know what happened. I got in a hurry, and I destroyed it, unintentionally. I robbed morning of its web, transition of its time, light of its own remorse, boy of his teen. The spider web is gone. But the lesson in delicacy lingers. Efficiency is not everything. Speed is often even less. Speed destroys things, like memories. Or passages. Or love. Or stuffed bears. Or cobwebs.

Sabbath keepers go slow. We go as slow as we possibly can. We keep sabbath by going slow. Which is to say that we can keep sabbath anywhere, anytime. All we have to do is slow down. And pause. And altar time.

*Bring us out of the house of bondage today, O God, into the house of freedom. Hear our thanks for the work of hands, and heart, and mind. Release us from the guilt we carry at not doing enough and never being done: bring us into the*

*grace of completion in incompleteness. Sabbath us, from time to time, even on the job. In the name of the true God. Amen.*

Cowley Publications is a ministry of the Society of St. John the Evangelist, a religious community for men in the Episcopal Church. Emerging from the Society's tradition of prayer, theological reflection, and diversity of mission, the press is centered in the rich heritage of the Anglican Communion.

Cowley Publications seeks to provide books, audio cassettes, and other resources for the ongoing theological exploration and spiritual development of the Episcopal Church and others in the body of Christ. To this end, it is dedicated to developing a new generation of theological writers, encouraging them to produce timely, creative, and stimulating publications of excellence, and making these publications available widely, reaching both clergy and lay persons.